Mahogany Nectar

TS Hawkins

iUniverse, Inc.
Bloomington

Mahogany Nectar

iUniverse books may be ordered through booksellers or by contacting:

iUniverse
1663 Liberty Drive
Bloomington, IN 47403
www.iuniverse.com
1-800-Authors (1-800-288-4677)

First printed by Wordclay November 23, 2010

Cover Design by Len Webb
www.lenakacruze.typepad.com

ISBN: 978-1-4759-7577-2 (sc)
ISBN: 978-1-4759-7578-9 (e)

Printed in the United States of America

iUniverse rev. date: 3/5/2013

Mahogany Nectar

Je vais exploser le baiser à votre conscience *Je vais exploser le baiser à votre conscience* Je vais exploser le baiser à votre conscience *Je vais exploser le baiser à votre conscience* Je vais exploser le baiser à votre conscience *Je vais exploser le baiser à votre conscience* Je vais exploser le baiser à votre conscience *Je vais exploser le baiser à votre conscience* Je vais exploser le baiser à votre conscience *Je vais exploser le baiser à votre conscience* Je vais exploser le baiser à votre conscience *Je vais exploser le baiser à votre conscience* Je vais exploser le baiser à votre conscience *Je vais exploser le baiser à votre conscience* Je vais exploser le baiser à votre conscience *Je vais exploser le baiser à votre conscience* Je vais exploser le baiser à votre conscience *Je vais exploser le baiser à votre conscience* Je vais exploser le baiser à votre conscience *Je vais exploser le baiser à votre conscience* Je vais exploser le baiser à votre conscience *Je vais exploser le baiser à votre conscience* Je vais exploser le baiser à votre conscience *Je vais exploser le baiser à votre conscience* Je vais exploser le baiser à votre conscience *Je vais exploser le baiser à votre conscience* Je vais exploser le baiser à votre conscience *Je vais exploser le baiser à votre conscience* Je vais exploser le baiser à votre conscience *Je vais exploser le baiser à votre conscience* Je vais exploser le baiser à votre conscience *Je vais exploser le baiser à votre conscience* Je vais exploser le baiser à votre conscience *Je vais exploser le baiser à votre conscience* Je vais exploser le baiser à votre conscience *Je vais exploser le baiser à votre conscience* Je vais exploser le baiser à votre conscience *Je vais*

OTHER TITLES BY TS HAWKINS

***

Sugar Lumps and Black Eye Blues
Confectionately Yours
Lil Blœk Book: All the Long Stories Short
The Hotel Haikus
Running Still Water

*****UPCOMING RELEASES*****

Black Suga: diary of a troublesome teenager
Poetry Schmo-etry
A Woman Scorned is a Woman Blessed
On My Knees Too Long: Prayers, Proverbs & Poems to GOD
Becoming Saturn: Counting Backwards from 60-30

Books/CDs available for purchase at all major online retailers
&
www.tspoetics.com

I'm her story...
A dalliance in her para-graphic penmanship
A literary illusion
Putrid pages caressing piqued language
Inked lyrics
Convincingly the well ran dry when penning the truth
Allowed to scribble moon-shined pictures
Tipsy shadows
Plastered bodies between sheets
Scripting miraged hope in sweat and sex
A fool, to play the main character
The vixen died as the ballpoint dug periods through each sentence
This isn't a murder mystery read over crumpets and tea
Not the Earl Grey with pinky pointed sophistication
Gazing through a highly bided screen play

I'm her story...
A dalliance in her para-graphic penmanship
Can't receive co-authorship
Nor editing credit
Dejectedly
I'm just a story
The outlined character traits
masquerading as a biological beginning
The title holding leatherette folds
A star in a melancholy melodrama
where silence seems so loud
Moving slowly through this silent picture
Wish to be stagnant with reason
Held hostage with words and images
Forced to steady pace
The mute object in the flip book
Flip pages like flipping clits to cum
Sticky parchment
Mending the remains of dignity

The quill left behind
Only still a moment

I'm her story…
A dalliance in her para-graphic penmanship
But revenge shall be mine to tell…

~Mahogany Nectar

ACKNOWLEDGEMENTS

***

For the love and support from
Sugar Lumps and Black Eye Blues and *Confectionately Yours*
readers

For those who continued to believe in the work and the arts

To Daddie Reagan

For lessons learned

For the diary of a *Troublesome Teenager*
who knew silence was never an option

DEDICATION

***

B.L.D
D.A.H
C.D.H
E.L
K.L.H.W
K.L.J

"240"

A.A.J

"To who I was"

JOURNAL OF CONSCIOUSNESS

***

CHAPTER THREE: *Sugar Lumped with Black Eye Blues*

AUTHOR'S NOTE

***

"Pardon, Garçon Serve Me Some Her...Again!"

The written word takes revenge on the author. Making the phalanges type truth and demanding answers for clarity and sanity; the writing takes the reigns. This is the work of **Mahogany Nectar**...digging deep, taking prisoners and leaving no subject matter unaddressed.

Within these folds, lovers, sex, friends, current events, enemies, mentors, revenge, relatives, ex-lovers, one nightstands, lust, stalkers, love and passersby are invited to dine at the lyrical dinner table. Feasting on double entendre, they all try to decipher who has cooked up what in the poems that lie ahead. Unbeknownst to them, they are just seasonings to an already brewing pot of conundrums and dreams. For even the author holds no control, she is the sous-chef and most times, the waiter, forced to serve her feelings to these guest on a silver platter. In this collection, no one goes un-devoured.

Mahogany Nectar pens an open-ended uncertainty. Unable to bake up dessert pleasantries, this is the official warning for who have a sensitive mental palette. Dibble and dabble sip-supple wordplay at your own risk as each sweet title hordes it own spice!

~With Nectar...

PREFACE

***

"With Iron Fist and Velvet Gloves..."

I've only met TS Hawkins once, while picking up tickets for a show I was reviewing. I can't say I remember much about that meeting, although she says she remembers both my daughter and me. And that makes sense. One thing I've learned since Ms. Hawkins asked me to write the preface for **Mahogany Nectar** is that she is all about noticing and connecting.

The majority of our interaction has been conducted through Twitter, the 140-character communication hub that's often dismissed as insubstantial, but rarely by those who have embraced its power as a tool for, yes, connecting. And so, Ms. Hawkins followed my feed, sent a message here and there to chat about Philly or theater, or Philly theater, and though our contact was brief, it quickly became clear that she was as genuine as she was enthusiastic about the arts.

Ms. Hawkins sent me her manuscript and again, I was struck by the themes of connection in her work. From the intensely personal, as in her poem *Ready 4 Me*, to *Deaf-iantly Struggling*, about the hugely public aftermath of the Haitian earthquake, Hawkins' own voice, fierce yet vulnerable, connects with her readers and asks them to look, however briefly, through her eyes.

What I like best about Hawkins' work is her honesty. Even when her poetry reflects difficult choices, humiliation or exploitation, she faces them full-on. Where some writers might couch their language in cagey metaphor, Hawkins is direct, her narrative clear. If she were standing in front of you, she would look you right in the eye.

Of course, much of her poetry lends itself to an in-person delivery, and while Hawkins' words come alive on the page, she can step to a mic with confidence, bunch up her words when necessary and unspool them at leisure. They're not always comfortable words, touched as they are by the effects of racism, homophobia, sexism, classism, first-worldism, but Hawkins' iron fist wears a velvet glove, and in YouTube videos of her various live performances, she sings about the failure of America's promise with a lovely lilt in her voice, a bright red flower poking from behind her ear. The politics may be hard, but she makes expressing them look easy.

Through this process, I learned that Hawkins started keeping a journal at 13, struggled with dyslexia as a child, and found a writing mentor in Temple University professor Dr. Kimmika Williams-Witherspoon. I also learned that she wanted my voice to appear alongside hers not just because she liked my writing, or wanted a journalist's validation, but because she valued my objectivity as a theater reviewer, and said she appreciated that whether or not I liked a dramatic piece, I left enough room for the audience to "decide their own theatrical destiny." Last season, I wrote a sharp critique of Dr. Williams-Witherspoon's monologue-driven docu-play *Shot!*, about gun violence in North Philadelphia, for the *Philadelphia Inquirer*. That Hawkins includes both Williams-Witherspoon and me among her creative influences--and doesn't mind going public about it--speaks volumes about her independent spirit and also, no doubt, her diplomatic skills.

I'm honored that Ms. Hawkins chose to connect with me, and you, the reader, ought to be honored as well. In **Mahogany Nectar**, Hawkins delivers her soul, as nectar-sweet as it is raw. That act requires a certain fearlessness few of us can muster; when Hawkins extends her hand here, you can rest assured she's offering to bring you on a loving, if turbulent, journey. Go on and take it with her.

Wendy Rosenfield
The Philadelphia Inquirer

Chapter One

Leaving the Nursery

The End of a Challenge

Dear Poetry:

At thirteen
You took my virginity
Smearing red splotches across sheets
Auto-correcting genetic flaws of comfortability
At eighteen
Thought I knew you through the strokes of others
At twenty-one,
Lost you
Let hazing liquids fog creativity
Attacking any spontaneity
At twenty-three,
Bound you between white folds
Claiming victory in release
And even though we have history
Without a clue of who you really are

Family Crest

Born: *Tamesha*

Middle name: *Shanay*

Hawkins: *A given name*

By an Irish, slave master's dick switch
With an English twist
This body lives a lie
Trying to be defined in Webster's puns
While parents find fun in a Baby Name book
Determine the bundle's destiny
Before getting the first look
This body
Having none
To do with it any longer
The search begins…

Queen Collection

Part 1:

Day one
Over-served your term
Ran miles to
Over-compensate for
The loss of your [lack of] better
Half. Accept my love for
Your strength through struggle

Part 2:

Every time common ground is found
Lost, is still the denominator
Over and over
I try to remain objective but
See that
Envy clouds your judgment to sincerity

Part 3:

Carefully monitored your entry
Here in this congested mass of
Angered, stifled and
Ridiculed inhabitance called
Life. Worked
Extra hard to protect you my
Sister. Now having complications watching you
Ease into adulthood.

Part 4:

Kindly
Enlighten the mind
Inside the mystery

Seen in you.
Humbled at your feet searching for
Answers to the connection

Part 5:

Kindred spirit
Immensely intrigued by the
Majesty of
Moving words to the declaration of
Independent thinking
Keen sense of insight
Attempting to duplicate, but struggling

Part 6:

Never let me fall
Although, too young to remember
Never let me die
Although, too young to fully appreciate the importance

Pearly Gates

Ever wonder that after death
You will see family members still waiting in line
Even though, they died years ago
Your relationship with them was poor on earth
Nevertheless, you have the urge to stand next to them
Realization hits that all of you are in the same situation
Negotiating for a better afterlife
Or maybe they delayed their entrance
To wait for you
So that appearing in front of gates together
Would be the first Family Reunion

Realization

Think of home
A place that has
Love overflowing...

Over flowing into trash bags
Placed on driveway's end
Sometimes not recycled properly
With a side order of leaves
That weren't picked up

Think about a place raging in flames
Of cookouts and housewarmings
Where an eight year old
Embellished tales
To gain the attention of Mommy's strangers
Because Daddy never gave her any

Think of a place where misery hung like wallpaper
Decorating success in drab
Where three little girls pretended to grow up happy

Think of home
A place that has
Love overflowing...

Overflowing with ritual to maintain order
Every Sunday bowing to powers to change the course in motion
Mondays designated for humming new tunes
Spent Tuesdays beating troubles with toe taps and grand jetés
On Wednesdays would gather round the piano
And stroke sadness through the keys of happiness
Thursdays and Fridays were field days
Tending to the ends of uncertainty
Volleying for a different roundabout
Only to use Saturdays for dusting out the weeks pain

Repeating it all, come Sunday morning

Think of a place where three little girls tried to make it work
Building the definition of "complete", "alright" and "will get there soon"
Wishing they knew back then,
That this is what Love is
And this is what Love was

Think of a place that's broken
Shattered pictures of memories left behind
The way they were
Before they changed
Before it changed them

Think of home
A place that has
Love overflowing...

Overflowing into a bucket of needs
Flooding
Necessities rising
Touching sockets
Electrocuting decency and order
Shocked that no one has answered the call for help

Think of a place where three little girls
Became women
Branching to tend to their own wants
Leaving one behind
Visiting sometimes
To bad news and decision time
Working separately on united issues
Wishing they knew back then that this...
This is what Love is
And this, is what Love was

Heaven's Little Girls

Little girls dream
Dream of adulthood
Dream of princes to save the day
Dream of wedding bells
Never that girl
Had a He-Man bedspread
Until Mama said to be more girly
Replaced by Strawberry Shortcake
With complimentary Tinkerbelle hygiene products
Ruffled socks and a thousand shades of pink

Little girls dream
Dream that one day they will no longer have to "play" house
Dream that the prince proposes on bended knee on Valentine's Day
Dream that happily-ever-after is tangible
Never that girl
Wanted independence
Wanted freedom
Wanted to be the answer to forever
"Whatever that meant"
Tried to understand tradition's practice
But always fell short
Realizing the picket fence will never be white
Or the possibility of not having the fence at all
Coping without the 2.5 children
A steady 401K
Dealing without the husband image
Raised toilet seats
"boxers or briefs"
Feeling no grief
It was never a goal
Wanting to live in the skin created
The dream
Equality

Little girls dream
Dream of ponies
Dream of wearing make-up before high school
Dream of being a lady
Never that girl
Played the part
For years
Against the will
Standing still
Maintained an image
Ultimately, hiding
Could never be “that girl”
No matter how hard the trying
Realizing that’s okay
For the first time

Birthday Card

Fragments of the brain
Left caterwauling release
Pounding on the grey matter
Turning it white
Frontal lobe reads blank
Like the pages forced to write on
To prove the opposite thought
"Blah"
Placed into centerfolds
The Rorschach rings clear
It's nothing
Like the moments lived
Too late to fix
Genetics has run its course
Failed at passing it
Time has come to gift-wrap the body
In bandages for safekeeping

(P)uberty

Between my parentheses
Lies this thing I dread
Semi to the colon
Its been known to drip unexpectedly
Like the girl in the 6th grade
Who stood up to find the end of her sentence
Ink stained the back of her britches

I loathe this thing
Between my parentheses
Wish to have the anatomy of an apostrophe
Hanging ten against the wind
Or easy breezy as a comma
No drama
No muss
No fuss
But I am stuck
With this polka dotted little fuck
Every 28 days it interrupts
The space between my parentheses
A sentence to be served
Until menopause takes its turn
Honestly, I'm over it
Its ruined all my fun
Point. Blank. PERIOD!

Can Hail Mary Save Me?*

I fucked my father

Fucked him so hard
To feel the closeness that my birth never allowed him to feel
Let his penis be the umbilical cord
To connect the space in our relationship
The first time we fucked
I was in between the sheets
Muddled with doubts
But let the uncertainty blanket my ass
As I pumped, humped, stroked into his favor
Inked
Red blotches marked new growing pains
The sheets couldn't hold the passion placed in its possession
Falling captive to his phallic penmanship
Signed away my innocence
As my virginity oozed through his dick
Who could predict the journey was just beginning

Let him bend me over
Doggie styled my way to beg for his affection
Acceptance from years of negligence
Pleaded to him to eat me out
To make room to find myself later in the process
With him, I learned the ways of karma sutra
But missionary was his favorite
Submission was the place I learned to find comfort
Strike three
Was at twenty-three
Had me ready to marry an incestuous situation
Could never cum to my senses
Because when we fucked, it was never for me
Thrusting for trusting
Pounding for appeasement
Stroking for freedom

Finding no clarity
I fucked my father

Routinely fucking to find a place in the vaginal mind
A moment that could make my clit tick
With pleasure to complete our relationship
But always cumming up dry
Crying won't wet the lips
They remain chapped
As I grasp for his last strokes of humanity
Constantly on my knees
But never having time to pray
Seconds spent suckling for his satisfaction
In hopes to get the same in return
Left to burn
Taking the shaft for his inadequacies
Now looking for closure
It's been two decades since my last confession
Depression has me wanting to start anew
Who knew
I would be fucked by every man
In search for my father's presence

Because I'm the black girl that settled for misogyny
When womanity became too tough
Let patriarchy mastodon sodomize growth
Strapped on the rainbow hue
Attempting to get a clue
Looking for comfort
Recreating endings
Hallucinating in fallacy
To compensate
I fuck my mother

Fuck her so hard to have her essence as my own
Sap her milk to nourish parching soul
Swallow her whole

A Mother Superior
Inferior
To the avarice
I leak in her rainforest
Scouring the forest floor
Reaping sour seeds of clarity
Sprouting nothing
Mother sits in the canopy
Watching
Thinking
Praying
While I prey on her nurturing practices
The understory
Holds the answers to who I am

So…
Who am I?
Am I the offspring of a higher power?
That has zilch to gain but heartache and pain
Should have nailed me to those planks
With four spokes
Therefore, I could have had a blueprint to my destiny
Wept at my own feet
Locked in a tomb
To give rebirth
A rise to sanity
Resend
Unblessed by the abyss
And zodiac constellations
Providing dim lighting to the future
Searching for something
Failing at the mission
To cope
I fuck my mother

Lay betwixt her breast and pillowed abdomen
To lie to myself

About safety I may never feel
Abandoned
Who will adopt this insecurity?
A waif
Left wavering in the winds of change
The bastard child
From a ménage a trois
Of Mother Earth
Father Time
A holey spirit

**from Confectionately Yours © 2009, extended for this publication*

Born Again

Stained glass
Used as holy water
Was baptized
A bastard
Unevenly yoked
Over easy
Grew up scrambled
An egg that should have been left for dead
Because Faith
Has no room
To be a muse
For a tepid soul

Fisting Water

Hannah Adams
With her brave new voice
Asked me
"Have I ever fisted water?"
With no response to render
Momentarily tendered poetic resignation
Speechless
        Inkless
                Thoughtless
Couldn't come to grips with the definition
But see now
Fisting water[1] is a downward ripple of insanity
Constantly pounding away at molecules that leak through the palm
Holding on to the last bit of possibility
Taking opportunity and slapping it in the face
Finding stability in a boundless discrepancy
It is the game fools play
...I lost
For fisting water has become a past time
                To pass time
        Waste time
I ask
"Have you ever strangled water?"
Release the breath from each hydrogen atom
Shake and squeeze until it felt the pain from within
Push it down
Letting it beg for mercy
Slowly recognizing that it was you that was drowning
For when you strangle water
It is you who is seeping to the underpinning of the abyss
Where life and death intersect
And you become the gravitational pull that holds them together

[1]Hannah Adams, Philadelphia poet wrote a poem entitled "Elements". With her permission, the usage of her "fisting water" passage created the title/theme for this poem.

Over It

Retrospect and Karma
Two bitches
Who wear pin stripped britches
Button-ups
Fedoras
With the occasional suspender highlight
Tough enough to have secluded lounge chairs at a gentlemen's club
And blow cigar rings around middle fingers
As if to say
"Je vais exploser le baiser à votre conscience"
Somehow
Met both of them in one day
Attempted to beat them
And lost
Left begging for mercy
If given the decision to do it all again
Would have chosen to be still born
Blue
At 6 pounds, 13 ounces
To have never looked at either in the eye

Natural Instincts

To run
To quit
To hurt
To work
To hide
To hate
To laugh
To flee
To cry
To jerk
To pretend
To dream
To suffer

I
Go against the grain daily

To be different
To love
To like
To care
To smile
To stay
To put the knife down
To put the gun down
To hold footing on the curb
To not be a disappointment

You
Try to help me

To be safe
To be trusting
To have feelings
To express
To hold

To embrace
To need
To want
To sing
To be joyous

But we
Are broken beyond repair

Fixing one another is complicated
If we are holding each other's pieces
And won't let go

I...
Became aware
Became stronger through weakness
Became open to see through my lesson

Will not be used
Will not be screwed
Will not be tampered with

Because I love you

Natural instincts
Have no boundaries
We have guns raised at each other's third eye
But the difference now...
Will not lower my weapon
If you won't!

Discovery

Alone
Is not a feeling of greatness
It is not honorable
Nor tolerable
And I will not follow the trend
So if I have to stalk my past to find the future
Then that's what I need to do...

Wind Blades

Ever try to catch a tornado
It's like running full force into to chaos with optimism
Caught in a whirlwind of endless possibilities
Where the centrifugal energy rains down on the soul
Numbing the mind
Swept up in the grey patterned wind chimes
Looking for clarity in spiraled turmoil
That was created by you
Tried to stop it from spinning out of control
Keep it from whipping around innocent bystanders
But no one looked out for me

Middle Passage

Vessel on loan
Collective tissue
Muddle muscle
Exposed bone
Existing
Risking
To tell a story
Experiencing life
For death
Drowning
For breath
Residing in purgatory state
…the search…
Still continues

TWA [Terminal with Angst]

Destined for greatness
With an expired passport
Seeking escape
Heart is on terror alert
Red flashes
Bright and stress ridden
A packed satchel of dreams
Standing between almost and impossible
Permanently deferred
Looking for comfort in bumpy roads
With R.T.S across the billet
Can't find refuge
If everything ever trusted
Never had my best interest

:nv:s:ble

Through the paper and pen
I breathe again

From birth
Phonetically mute
Couldn't type a rhyme
Recite a line
Scribble a muffled afterthought
The soul
Bought and sold
In the womb
A tomb to creativity
The path created
Wasn't for me
Wanting to plea
"WHO KNEW
THAT THE BIRTH OF ME
WAS MY DEATH"
And would spend
Lifetimes to be reborn

Through the paper and pen
I breathe again

Spit concern with flair
Gaining confidence
Daring challenges
Silencing those who chose
To keep me quiet
From birth
Told everything
How to eat
When to sleep
Where to stand
How to plan

Why continue…

Through the paper and pen
I breathe again

The conductor
Driving force
Of my own course
Torture
Was etched upon the throat
Saved in tandem by the dictionary and thesaurus
Regretted being born
But thankful for reincarnation
This carnage of flesh
Was laid to rest

Through the paper and pen
I breathe again

Questioning ignorance
Writing for substance
Looking for civics
Knowledge drenched ink
Wrapped in parchment
The placenta
Releasing positive energy
Striking the poet's umbilical cord
Shaking away discontentment
Using words to evoke harmony

Because through the paper and pen
I breathe again

Allergies during Harvest Time

Sneezing and wheezing
Blowing the nose to release your toxins
Allergic to your pollination
Rag weeds of uncertainty
Dust mites of indecency
Rendering the response
"God Bless You" in my direction
When it is you
That much blessings are required

End of a Cycle

It is over…

Not going to cry any longer
Its been long enough
Not going to carry this burden
Its been heavy
Embracing breath
The ability to breathe beyond the realm of the lung span
Inhale everything positive about existing

It is over…

Not going to weep
The presence of desperation no longer smells sweet
Sleepless nights
Won't be the whore monger leaving stress on the dresser
Not being able to stand in the morning
Weak from rolling in midnight satin tears
Passion filled depression
Blanketing the woes of the day
Who knew bringing work home
Was more than just a one night stand

But it is over…

Lay restful in a pressure-less existence
Can walk the streets
Head in the upright position
Knowing the current position in life
Feels comforting understanding peace
Rooftops awaiting this voice of reason
To scream
Laugh
And be merry
Enjoying something

Once taken for granted

So glad
It is over!

A Moment in Time

With eyes wide shut, I
Put to rest misconception
Of hero work. I

Removed the "S" from my breast
And took the day off for self.

Memoirs to the Mirror pt. 5

Saw the reflection
Kissed it, told it "I'm Sorry"
Will love you today

Tomorrow and the next day
And the next day to follow!

Ready 4 Me

The look in your eyes says,
"Immediately be mine"
The swagger in your sway says
"In my own time"

And I say,
"I will wait..."

Will wait in the arms of another
While you find your way home
Will wait while being the twinkle in someone else's eyes
Will wait by the phone
In long distance conversations
Lingering walks with sunsets
Cuddling in stardust
With a Sunday picnic made for two
I will wait for you
In the gaze of a new lover
Want you
When you are ready for me

The look in your eyes says,
"Immediately be mine"
The swagger in your sway says
"In my own time"

And I say,
"I will wait..."

Will wait while walking down the aisle
Looking straight ahead at a face that is not yours
Will wait for you to interject
Even if there is silence
I will wait...
Will wait in grocery lines

Hoping that the hand that grazed my shoulder was yours
Saying its time to move forward
Will wait like a latchkey child
With a parent running minutes late
With certainty that they are in route
Receiving a hug so huge
So tight with apology
That tardiness will never happen again

The look in your eyes says,
"Immediately be mine"
The swagger in your sway says
"In my own time"

And I say,
"I will wait..."

In this non-linear space
This cosmetic journey
Where yesterday is today
And today was six months ago
Wait like our souls are hoping that the flesh catches up
For they said "I Do" centuries prior
Will wait like transients asking for change
World-order itching for peace
And Hope looking for salvation

I will wait...
I will wait...
I will wait...
Want you
When you are ready for me

I Am

I
am the misunderstanding that circles your denial
I wonder when those eyes wide shut, open to acknowledge the sounds
I hear as the glass ceiling crumbles at your feet
I am greater than your expectations

I
pretend to swallow insecurities through shots of liquored love
I feel its wrong but
I touch the soul with inebriated fingers
I worry that's the only stroke to my satisfaction, unfortunately
I am the misunderstanding that circles your denial

I
understand the belittling rendered to elevate your inferior inclinations
I say nothing for fear of being alone
I dream to awake from self-loathing trance
I try to convince the consciousness to wage war on this emotional battlefield
I hope to win for
I am greater than your expectations!

Chapter Two

Soap Box Auction Blocked

Downsized

B *r* o *k* e *n*
Halves wishing to be whole
Only worth a fourth of the time to be around
Spending an eighth of the moment in truth
Wallowing in the sixteenth fragments of a future
Muddled in the thirty-second themes to appease
Barely hanging on
Aware of obstacles masquerading as unconditional love
The head lies on a pillow of denial
With fear of being misused and forgotten
B r *o* k *e* n
Settling for the mediocrity of self
Servicing others for a whim and a prayer
That maybe
Just maybe
Working hard enough to be whole
Can cover the rose-colored illusions of existing

Deaf-iantly Struggling

Haiti,
A hormonal entity being bid on.
Insignificant hoarder of demolition.
Time ticks as funds trickle down through dick-less majesty
In time, Mother Nature will think about apologizing for
Humanity.
A never-ending story underwritten as a comedic tragedy.
Instead of an action plan, reaction
Takes the reigns, pats itself on the back and
I am no better.
Handwriting change as poetic rhyme that mimics
Apathy. Disillusioned to devastation.
I am the product of commercial sensationalism.
Tempting emotions with wordplay. When did
It come to this?
Having complications
Appeasing tangibility. *"Just can't feel it yet"*.
It shouldn't be this way.
Toe tapping around the issue, placing
Images on mute.
Hearing no evil.
A silent deviant,
Incapable of grieving even when
Toddlers grasp for nothing, for
I am the emptiness they cleave onto!

CrypTonite

A cape-less heroine
Caught in a wind tunnel of nepotism with lack luster performance
Wondering when the next shoe will drop
Expose the toes of segregated ideologies
The conclusion
She is broken
In trying to create her own stimulus plan
She allowed her essence to drown in the sea of no return
Told to perish by water
The flesh rots under the waves
While the soul gets reborn in the undertow
Maintained the shuck and jive
Wallow in nonsense
So eager to feel something
She, noosed by the paycheck
Left dangling as a symbol of good work ethic
In retrospect
Should have just bent over and remained silent
Docile
A numb-nut

This cape-less heroine has aged
With pained heart and bleeding pockets
Willing to do it again
To die for the last drop of love
Death of reality is strongly approaching
Seeping into the dark of night
Bidding farewell to what could be and once was
She retires
Tired
Expired upon the desk of success
Held up by lies
Deceit
And neglect of self

This cape-less heroine
Has written epitaph on her birth certificate
The afterbirth
Her coffin
The womb
Her tomb
And she came forth anyway
A martyr for others wounds
"Jesus ain't seen the half"
"Thought He paved the path to selflessness"
Must have skipped a chapter
The heroine niche-d it first
Took every beating without grimace
Still being told she is worthless
She deteriorates in the arms of hypocrisy
Cradle rocked to ill-fated office tunes
Eased to comfort through the false smiles of colleagues
Pressed on
Until pressed out
Surrendered
Broken
Broken
Broke in shards not worth repairing

This cape-less heroine
Removes the "S" from her breast
Weeps at her funeral
For she was the only guest in attendance

The Soul's Life

She sells seashells
By the sea shore
This sea whore
No more than four
With shovel and pail
Try to hail parents
For the affection and joy of summer fun
Under the sun
Interrupting their sport
This sea whore
That sold seashells
By the sea shore
Tried once more
Inching to the waterfront
Removing the suit
Bathing in nudity
Tossed the shovel and pail
Inhaled the salt water
Spoke prayers through murky weeds
A non-retractable deed
"Pay her the attention she needs"
So this plea
Is not the epitaph for your seed

Closing In

Dear Fool:

Hannibal Lector treats feelings with more dignity
Sodomizing the lexicon for the last time
Wrapping lingual dexterity about the hands and abdomen
Committing the self to safety

Umm, Interesting

In order to spit game to you
Must turn my age of 25
To 52…

Because the wisdom doesn't match the vocal stroll
Though the soul is old
And attracted you to me
But due to mental math
You decided to subtract you from me
So us could never make we
If you took time to add my wisdom to your age
Multiply three times
My ciphered lines against your one tracked degree
You'd see
That I'm actually your elder
Would respect you more than you did me

Can't believe
That in order to spit game to you
Must turn my age of 25
To 52…

To be on your physical level of understanding the essence of me
See mentally
With one conversation
I've out grown you
Aced your basic principles
Solved your riddles
Though pivotal
Still trivial and hypocritical
Your esquire expired
It's time for you to get re-certified in my pages
Open me up to see what you missed
Possibly ditched
Because you got twisted up in a numerical switch

That left you ignorant
Callus and penny-less
Broke
Broken
Let me be your student loan
Make the interest worth your while
My style will have you wishing to complete me in four years

Can't believe
That in order to spit game to you
Must turn my age of 25
To 52…

When in actuality
I'm the one who gave birth to you
Once the placenta shattered
You stopped seeing the truth
Got too big for your britches
Gazing at reality with rose colored lenses
Hiding behind your Benz's
And I'm the one that needs to grow up
That's messed up
Let me stuff you with my seed
Re-create me in your womb
So you can feel what greatness is like
Scribble within the lining of your center
In hieroglyphics
The truth about yourself
This moment
This fragment of time
So that when you push me out for the world to see
You'd think twice about telling me

That in order to spit game to you
Must turn my age of 25
To 52…

To blanket the insecurities
You've become accustomed to

Poison

Dear Fool:

Stop talking!
Your condescension builds a ladder,
So I may always climb above you.

The Plantation Has A First Name...

Tall tales drape tree limbs
Bearing fruit
Never tasted
Assumed tainted as they fell to the earth
Soaking their seeds in cold rustic winter soil
Hoping to grow better than the assumptions consumed by their ancestors
For they were the good **Blacks**
Referred by the right neighbor
Denied by the left
Treated like overgrown weeds
The poisoned poppies of the community
Where block parties blocked relationships from forming
Rumored that corruption was the house's foundation
Where they rest their aspirations
*"We never had good **Blacks** here"*
They are all the same
"Brown tones pretending to own homes"
Where white sheets make rules
Fooled to believe a new day is risen
Imprisoned by the American Dream
The REM cycle holds the reigns
Even in the safety of the white picket fence
They can never call it home
Its just woods and lakes
Where they hang their heads
Drown in goals
Struggling to die in peace

The P/Y/T

Stuck in a middle ground
Where plastic dolls and gas bills
Don't mix with anti-depressants
Punished
Spent years trying to grow down
Since I grew up to quick
Developing a brave new voice
But still having to keep silent
"Stop telling me I'm too young"
Using ooh's, ahh's
To pacify
Your attraction towards me
Dumb-ing me down to the most finite degree
Distracting the possibility of you and me
Wish the situation was reversed
So you can fix what you're saying
Displaying ignorance
Masquerading it as age old intelligence
A costume that doesn't fit
Cherish me
Respect the foundation
This shallow-ness is causing strife

Caught in the middle
Where Wisdom is the first name
And Immaturity the last
Blamed for being childish if to place you on blast
Patted on the back if the high road is taken
Letting the situation remain in the past
Where does that leave the soul to lay its head?
Sick and tired of the standards
That doubles as egotistic and simplistic
Honoring the words of my essence
Denying the shell the embrace
Because an age difference

That's a disgrace
We speak the same language
But you've blackened the berries
No longer sweet juice
Can't produce seeds
Now've become too old
In my soul
Jaded
Too ancient to be persuaded
Was denied
At the tender age of 25
All because these thoughts and feeling
Where before their time
Now lain in the crypt
Can't recite any lines
Nor rhymes
You killed growth's process
Had me living a tainted lie
For what
To ease the lusting savage in your private place
To turn tricks on your mental dick
Because it cummed to quick
With my poetic wit
And it made you sick
That this 25 soon to be 26
Year old
Made your britches swole
With her intellect

Memoirs to the Mirror pt. 2

When the tear falls
Who is it for?

When the heart breaks
Who is it for?

When the soul aches,
Who is it for?

Who is it for?
When the body heaves for clarity

Who is it for?
When the hands grasp for honesty

Who is it for?
When pain is caged through omission

When the wrists bleed
Who is it for?

When the rope snaps
Who is it for?

When there is a scream for help
Who is it for?

Who is it for?
When weeping water-drops splash upon cased pillows

Who is it for?
When the bubbling rage is hotter than a volcanoes whisper to the dawn

Who is it for?

When nothing equals what's left

Not worth the afterthought
Not worth the foresight to be let go
Not worth the time

So what was it for?

A Life Choice

Murder
Murder
On her walls
She's not a parent after all

Reason
Reason
Let's be fair
She saved a zygote from despair

Murder
Murder
On her walls
She's not a parent after all

People
People
Shut your mouth
The soul, already filled with doubt

Murder
Murder
On her walls
She's not a parent after all

Judgment
Judgment
Please don't stare
This wasn't done as a dare

Murder
Murder
On her heart
She has already fallen apart

So…

People
People
Shut your mouth
Her soul already holds that doubt

Pay the Bill

Starting to feel vacant
Opened a tab
To block a void

"Fill the glass bartender"

Don't skimp
Vodka over flow
Drown in rum
Aching for southern comfort
Don't need it on the rocks
Chill is not what needs to be felt
Serve it straight up
Like it, dirty
Add three olives
So classiness can be sought

"Fill the goddamn glass bartender"

It's empty…
It's empty…
It's empty…
I'm drained
Will let you know when the limit has been hit

"À votre santé!"

The Pulse is Mourning

Maya talks about the "pulse of morning"
But she ain't seen Philadelphia at 5am
It's like a freeze frame
Of sudo- success and malice
Where pigeon crowned birds search for sustenance
From human remains and earthly decay
The mastodon then, had a better outlook
There is talk of brotherly love
Sisterly companionship
Racial equality
And neither exist where it matters
Hunkered down in the hustle and bustle
Common decency takes a backseat
In a mini-van
Car-pooling to straight jacketing workloads
Some of those pools were still **WHITES ONLY**
Segregated justice arriving on the heels of hijacked hydrants
On a 90 degree day
Busting the flesh of civility
See, from Jena to Philly
People still Rock to the tunes of deviance
Leaving the River and the Tree
Holding the banner for their ignorance
This new day dawning
Has already set
For the sun can never shine on theory
Clearly
The only thing constant in the world is change
Since the only change seen jangles in the cups of the destitute
We live a life of variables that don't play fair

Dinner with Truth

Zealously attempted to change the hands of time
Yielding reason with
Xeroxed
Wisdom coddled by a fork
Vexed tongue. Vetted
Under preconceived notions
That was, too, truckled by fallacy. Leaving
Saturnine, head buckled between thighs. No longer
Refulgent with hope
Questioning existing in a world of
Poor promises and
Open heartache
Not wanting to ask for help, the
Mouth waning in malapropism,
Lingers in
Kindred dreams of a future unforeseen
"Just move on with celerity and alacrity"
Is the diktat rendered back. Slightly
Hindered by the harsh tones
Got a grip on reality
For a moment
Everything can't have smooth transitions
Delectation doesn't describe all actions. Some
Carom against the breastplate
Breaking wind from the lungs, trying to erase it
All to never feel it again.

"Life will never be easy..."

Untitled

Wisdom
Comes from old men
In coffee shops
With freshly unfolded newsprint
Conversation drenched in caffeinated ink
Verbiage waving in the air
As banners of knowledge, pride and political rebellion
Rimmed lenses atop a bridged nose
With each phrase
It turns itself up to reprimand idiocy and lies

Truth
Comes from old Black men
In barber shops
Where justice is balanced
Shape-ups and haircuts serve as free weights
Tipping the world's inadequacies
To equality
With the swish of a hair brush and whisk of hair clippers
Silently they run the world
No one hears them
They are debunked as common and uneducated

Deception
Comes from the mouths of the ill-informed
Wrapped in personal shoppers and hair stylists
Gossip is the news of the day
Highlighting the ups and downs in the mundane
Secretly wishing they knew what life felt like

Redemption
Stems from the weary
Sipping freedom through broken glass
The blood red vodka
Leaves the palette contemplating unreasonable reason

While standing on bar stools
The mind secretes
The wallet depletes
And the soul finds sobriety in the long walk home

Denial
Smiles from the mouth of child that lies
To uphold parental self-esteem
The beginning to the end of anything meaningful
For humanity remains saturated in the fear of reality
Black fibs vesting as growth spurts
White lies seamlessly stroke pubescent dreams
Where the grey ones coat the non-negotiable truth

I
Am a youth dwelling on a wish and a prayer
Denial signs its penmanship on the birth record
Redemption and **deception** branch the family tree
Decide to go against tradition and unite with **truth**
A civil union worth fighting for
Desire to labor for **wisdom**
To make up for mistakes made

Taking Flight

Impaled by dogma
Unable to see clearly
As the crimson trickles downward
Seizing faith
Nailed to the right of the Father
Realized it is staged for the ratings of others
PG: G-O-D
Where "T's" are crossed
To be misused
Biblical teachings
Rolled into balls
Hurled at those looked upon as different
Grenade-d
Administering prayer in the form of pink mist
Taking ritual to the 21st century
Bombed
Who knew belief was the new terroristic threat?

OutSpoken

In 2005
Allegedly committed a crime
In trusting lust
Lusting after a man across the bar
From a far he looked like a good catch
Not knowing later that he was going to snatch the snatch
Having personal essence take the rap
Serving sentencing unjust
From every future thrust
Caress and flirtatious glance
"I'm the victim locked behind bars"
Scarred
Marred
Maimed
In pain to be intimate with another
Was innocent when he slipped it in
Co-horsed to disrobe
Remain silent
He stole...
Still shackled by the imagery
That permeates the psyche
Subconsciously
Imprisoned for his actions
"Get my vagina off death row"
Pardon it
Pardon it
Pardon its appearance
For its been untouched by human hands
Jammed by strangers plans
Fort Knox-ed by crippling demands
Three hots and a cot
Can't nourish it
Weight lifting won't strengthen it
This caged bird won't sing
Muffled

Need society to understand
This is not the radical rantings of a statistic
Not simplistic
Don't take this voice
Reduce it to random percentages
Don't take this voice
Diminishing it to phallic indulgences
Was whole
Until he took the vaginal soul
And put a hole in it
Trying to get off on good behavior
Where was the savior
When Please, Stop, and No
Were 3 commandments that remained un-followed
Hollowed out by keeping the story within
Now, telling it not for sympathy
For justice
For the unspoken
For the abused and misused
For change
Open nation's eyes
To these acts of violence
Silence, no longer the cuffs that bind

Colored in the Box

Crayola tells a story
In preschool
Teacher displays progress
She outlines the hands
She outlines the feet
Learn to color within the lines
A mother's pride
Strides the length of her face
At young age
Understood advancement happens
When staying in the designated space

At the elementary level
The lesson repeats
For the classic Thanksgiving tale
The historic dinner
Feast of humanity
"Later learned that it was a lie"
Followed the assignment
Outline the hands
Outline the feet
Phalange represents the turkey's meat
The feet
The potato mold for the cornucopia
But something is amiss
Understood the assignment before it was explained
It felt innate
The tracing of the feet
A symbol of segregation
Now a Crayola based lesson
A continued expression of lies and oppression

We traced our feet
Those brown toes never touching the merchandise
Those same toes that plowed the fields

Bore the ache of the freedom train
Built the nation
Marched for justice
Not permitted to sample an Oxford
A crummy shoe
Or new church boots
Not wanting to risk the "No Return Policy"
We traced our feet
Outlined the possibility of a perfect fit
To fit the status quo
We traced our feet
Stooped to the arrogance of the ignorant
To live in their insecurities
Tired of living within the lines
Succeeding by their guidelines of mediocrity
We traced our feet

Next our bodies
Concrete street tombstones
Outline self-hatred
Bloodstains remain
Chalk residue claims our existence
We believed their lies
Raised ourselves to trust their creed
Glocking nines
Because our enemy is dressed to the nines
Die-hards to the basketball
Because practice makes perfect
Yet draw straws for education
Because it doesn't pay quick
Thinking we're slick
Can't get it up
For working full time
But, there's no impotence
To a halfway hustle
Need to value ourselves
Uplift the family

Give “wifeys” wedding rings
Leave the baby mama drama to the screenplays
Two can play that game
Tired of waiting to exhale
Inhaled enough disrespect
To raise the slaves that jumped the ships
Only to have them turn over in their watery graves
Asking why
The continuance of nonsense
Defines a lineage
They self sacrificed to protect
Take time
Rejuvenate the community
Bless neighbors
Turn the cheek to negativity
Stop the thievery
Stealing the existence of us
Dragging ourselves to the most wanted list
Waiting behind bars
For the scale of justice
To balance out
Shortchanging progress
Can’t afford to go backwards
No bailouts to parachute into our holes
President can’t even stimulate our stagnant stimulus
Won’t continue
To outline the hands
Outline the feet
Reality…
Is no longer a Crayola based lesson

Happy Hour

One drink
Two drink
We drink
You stink

Start the round with Sex on the Beach
Rekindling memories
Rolling on Long Islands
Knocking back top shelves of the unattainable
Fantasies
Between the liquor and ice chucks
Then Gin
A tonic that's toxic enough to make a clean slate
Only to consume a Lemon Drop
A shot of symbolism
Sour mixing with sugars
Jumping off the rim of the glass
Into the mouth
Going down smoothly
A misapprehension of rationality
Because everything is Dark and Stormy

One drink
Two drink
We drink
You stink

Clarity shows up around...
Round four
Pulls up a chair
Glares into the eyes
Removes the beverage
Pays the tab
Then walks alongside on the route home
"Walk it off..."
The answer doesn't rest on coasters
Don't leave the soul on the rocks
Not the way to "chill out"

Memoirs to Mirror pt. 4

Love is like contraband

Like standing on street corners
The office space
Where colleagues continually pocket the office equipment
Nickel bag here
Dime piece there
Using handshakes as an exchange for indecency
Palms lined with sweat and greed
Because the only way to move up
Is by stooping lower than imagery can color

Love is like contraband

Like a kilo spooning cannabis
Under a midnight sky
In the backyard of a brothel
Or a commune for those more dedicated

Love is like contraband

Like a bride walking down the aisle
And the pastor's wife chuckles at the gown
Knowing that the dress should have been ecru
Guests blinded by the white
The bride
A virgin to her soul
Looked to the groom
As the words, "I Do" escaped the palette
Squeezed the hand of the Maid of Honor
Caressed in satin amethyst
For the bride found her Queen instead

Love is like contraband

Like groping around dark alleys
Sliding up an un-expecting dress slip
Taking naivety
Swaddling it with prostitution
Leaving dignity on the nightstand
Creating night terrors
Fear, the new flesh monger
Making lurid surroundings comforting
To shallow fantasies

Love is like contraband

Like saying the words prematurely
Backpedaling the emotion
Pretending time will erase the letter formations
Swarming around a lover's thoughts

Love is like contraband

Like an adopted youth
Returning to the orphanage
The new parents couldn't handle the stress
And the youth found comfort in abandonment
The original arrangement may have been best
The grass on the other side always looks greener

Love is like contraband

And running away from it
Won't be the safety net
To catch the misunderstanding
That that has other's serving life sentences on death row

B4 Technology*

Before technology ran amuck
People took time to sign on the dotted line
Sincerely
Fondly
Respectfully
With love
For you admiration
Could be displayed
On the page
The ink and quill
Tilled the soil
Of every growing thought process
Extending the energy
To get to know one another better

Before technology ran amuck
We could pick up the phone
Sprinted to dial numbers
Listened to each other's day
Focused so deeply on the connection until we hear the pin drop
Did long distance with AT and T
For the touch tone T and A
Wouldn't let miles disconnect the service of the relationship
Now texting is all the rage
Its friend Twitter keeps the personal stats for the day
The new rejection hotline is Blackberry Messenger
Send "Dear John" letters with ease then blocking the user once it's done
Because dumping you with only 160 strokes is no fun
Not bold enough to face the book
Or type it in MySpace
Settling to be mediocre
Hiding behind the wave of the future

Before technology ran amuck

Waited with baited breath
That the carrier pigeon didn't get pigeon held by changing wind formations
Hope that those men on horseback
Didn't get backed up
Clutching the message after months have passed
Sending an S0S to the world
Get the message in a bottle
Praying that the note is not lost at sea
Casting away the letter formations that need to make it through

Before technology ran amuck
Traveled months on the wagon trail to find you
Suffered cholera, malaria
All disease
To please
Entertain the thought that the words and feelings will get to you
Now getting people somewhere aka GPS
Maps routes that leads to wrong exits and dead ends
Only good for its programmed programming
Yet every car has one
Despite the flaws
And have the gall not to leave the driveway until it's been rebooted
Ready to go
No more basking in the glory of longing
All is lost
In this fast paced world
Where sexting is cool
Video phones putting Gchats to shame
Playing mental games with the internet
AIMing to please
"Get it quick" schemes
Living by iCal as the new pen pal
Emailing chain letters of *"God will bless you"* if you send it to 12
Or send it to 9 and your money problems will be solved one last time

Before technology ran amuck

Used to read books for research
Having the Dewey decimal system guide the way
Now wasting away hours
Being witted by the wikki 's "pedia"
Boggled by Google
Asking Jeeves
Bing
Getting peeved
That your final paper still received a "C"
All because you didn't go the library and read
Relied solely on the XP
And High Speed
To feed the greed of getting an "A"
No one polices the sites
To determine if the information is right
Yet you faithfully recite and quote
Denote
The findings in the bibliography
Claiming research on half thoughts and opinions of others

Before technology ran amuck
We had common sense
We're struck dumb by YouTube
Being scantily clad on Downelink
But want everyone to be LinkedIn
So folks can Instagram your mullet resume
Because your professional front likes to party in the back
When did we become so whack?
We are our own weapons of mass destruction
With a Bluetooth gnawing on the ears
Razor flipped phones
Our BlackBerry's stormed
And uploaded to the HP's
With iPods being the new worm in the Apple
Sending leeching synapses to the frontal lobe
Allowing technology to replace something so sacred
Humanity

Even handshakes are Palm Pre-ed
Droid
Void
"iTouch only apps"
Half living through ATM fees
Direct deposits
Automated messages
Self-checkout
Vending Machines
All because we don't want to take the extra steps to face one another

Before technology ran amuck
Could remember the sound of your voice
Interpersonal skills laid to rest behind a voice mailing system
Though I am laying right next to you
iPad my pillow with just enough energy to tweet you
"Good Night"

**appeared in Verseadelphia, published by New City Press © 2010.*
Originally performed at the NJPAC in 2009.

Bulls Eye

Nigger Moment

Should have left me a Nigger
Shackled by my own insecurity
Chains jangling like a baby carousel above my head
Providing sugar plum nonsense
Lulling me to night terrors
And daydreams
Brain farting what freedom could smell like
This American Apparel
Is moth infested
It adorns my back
Heavy atop the shoulder
Holding this pile
This boulder
This American Dream
That slashed through the Pearl of Africa
To fill the Gap
In what was left behind
Your milieu never suited me

Should have left me a Nigger
This American Pie is a bit stale
Without enough Lagers nor ales to cleanse the bitter palette
Lie dormant
Drunk in the happenstance
That maybe
When you gave me a free ticket on the cruise ship
CORRECTION: Slave ship
You would look out for me
But it was my fault for not reading the fine print
That "I would never be free again"
The saving grace was that I was light enough
Bright enough to work in the House
But even the house
Didn't have any Representatives that looked like me
Continually on hands and knees

Attempting to please those who would never care
Bought and sold by Capitalistas
Because Democracy is slowly becoming a hypocrisy
So I remain in the middle
A passage that never had its Rights read
But mirandized for double standards

Should have left me a Nigger
Because even as a Black Panther
I was just a wild cat
With no place to call, home
A stray
Being lead astray
With violence and leather fringe
Binging harmony
Leaving anorexic dreams deferred in fickle legacy
Surprised that the KKK and we, were enemies
In most cases, we dotted the wrong "i's"
Crossed our own "t's"
And set them a blaze for the world to see
The only difference between them and we
We were too poor to buy the sheet
We still kill our own peace
With sheets of parchment
Titled degrees
That we use to keep us "separate but equal"
And had the gall to yell at Jim Crow
When the fare is paid
We still take the backseat
Constantly bringing up the rear
Or giving up our rearing principles
Noosing our youth to bad habits, illiteracy and stupidity
Knowing we are one tree away from swinging to our demise
Jena wasn't the first time we heard of this news
Just the first time in the millennium we decided to pay attention

Should have left me a Nigger
Drifting on the island seas
Believing me to believe that my ancestry
Wasn't birthed in the womb of the Motherland
Being upset when someone titles me as Black
When I wish to live the deception of being a Caribbean
And while standing on American soil
Pledge to God and the Almighty dollar
That there is "justice for all"
Who succumb to the monotony of the B.S. of A
A…Land in which we built
B…Rebuilt thanks to Katrina's reign
C…Where reparations is a taboo word
With an apology seesawing with amnesia
While playing rock…paper…scissors…
SHOOT, we lost our place in line to the Jews
And their suffrage didn't even happen here
But took their "ghetto" terminology and made it our own
Suppose freedom is not what we are looking for?
Just a hollow cost
For a cold shower and a final resting place

Should have left me a Nigger
Because remember…
"Its shake and bake and I helped"
Helped mammy the master's youth
With nothing more to lend to our own
Yet show scorn when the prisons are filled with our own
Because the streets and cartoon cable stations raised them
Morals taught by Wild E. Coyote
Mothering by SpongeBob
With his pineapple under the sea
And when our children
Dumpster dive in search for their parental guidance
Then we show a backbone to the government
When its way too late
Our treasures become tombstones

And the cycle repeats one more time
When the government called our bluff
And put our babies on the front line
What made it worse?
They were more at more harm and danger
When they "asked and told"
That their soul
Belonged to another that had the same anatomy as them
We gave the nation weapons of mass destruction to kill them
Only to run to the little comforts of our Bibles
Those same words used for prayer to save their lives
Now lancets to their eternal downfall
And we continue to hide in the lies
To say Leviticus foretold it anyway

Should have left me a Nigger
Then I knew where I stood
On action block
Poked and prodded
Nude
Hung
A barren strange fruit

"Nigger Moment" first published in Cipher This on November 6, 2009

For Phil, Lest We Forget

Like turpentine on the spine
You irritate
The nonsense you spit
With bark weaker than bite
The height of your stance
The observance of your gate
Irks the fiber of the being equip for understanding
No judgment
Just truth seen through vaporous gaze
A medicinal elixir reminiscent of kerosene
Stroking a fire for no good reason
It's better when you're silent
Escaping the utterance of chaos
Perched upon the tongue
Creating halitosis
Stepping away
The toxins emanating from your mouthpiece
Wishing to have met you unscented
Untainted by the debauchery dangling from your tonsils
Speak no longer
You never really had anything to say

Chapter Three

Sugar Lumped with Black Eye Blues

Mnemonic Optical Phenomenon

Pulling teeth to
Really understand why there
Is immense
Discussion over the most
Elementary subject matters.

"Its just sex..."

Thesis

Sun-kissed by black valor with chin hold accompaniment
Past transgressions flood
Cupped phalanges to keep emotions from overflowing
"what will the wife say"
When the smelling salts of desperation
Linger on shirt's collarbone
Each button mapping routes that led parts to stray from home
To say it meant "nothing"
Would mean nothing
Digressed bodies
Suspended vows
Unioned this moment for the posterity of memory
Each bend and fold coursing lament
Discourse
Disrobe
Divulge, for this is Scarlet's essay
Despite marking on both sheets
Rendered 'A'
Worn for effort
On a job well done…

Prenatal Halitosis

Can smell pregnancy on your breath
When going down on me
You place your tongue on my clit’s lips
To spit game
Only births more problems that I have with you
Can't be bound to the appendage of us
When us was never part of the equation
Though a roll in the hay is something desperately desired
I simply can't indulge this temptation
Because I
Can smell pregnancy on your breath

Hound

Dear Fool:

Bark up another tree...
That pussy is occupied!

On Repeat

Sunny breasts up
She sleeps through the dawn
Watch her consume the day
As her lungs rise and fall
The gleam of possibilities glistens on her temples
Like skipping stones
Making its way to her eyes
Finally open to greet mine
The midnight concubine
That illuminates a surprise
Allowed by her liquid courage
Wrapped in each other's afternoon
We make the day non-linear
Its better this way...

Ugggh…This Again?

Waking up to you
Would be a great dream come true
But reality...

Is harsher than fallacies
So, don't want to wake up now.

Should I Cook You Breakfast?

Gave birth to freedom
One night
That led to morning
Left mourning
Exiting on the next midnight train
Leaving me
Now, a single parent
To a newborn identity

Melodious Perplexity

In tune to one instrumentalist
One stroke
One constant octave
A musical improvisation
That produces an original opus with every performance
Lately
With celerity
Someone else has been plucking the strings
Creating a dissonance
Beats slamming together
Determining to make intense sounds
But relying on sheet music
Following note formations
Aiming for G major
Trying to be sharp
Stuck
Being flat
In the bellow of another
This overture
An unusual score
An unpredictable concerto
Has the body aching for an encore
Enjoying the strumming
The cacophony
The atypical composition
But
Is it alright to switch conductors
Before intermission
Knowing the relief can't stay for curtain call

17 Syllables

A haiku isn't enough
Cinquain's create pain
And free verse
Too epic
Making the reader narcoleptic
The thoughts are speechless
Can't reach the plateau of innuendo
Palms sweat
Nerves a wreak
Just say *"Yes"*
The question is understood

A Vow

For
Better

For
Worse

For
Unlawful
Carnal
Knowledge

I
Will

I
Do

Must
Choose
You
To
Be
Whole

Once

More

Note Taken

I wrote her a note...
Crafted blueprints to my heart
A simple plan
But it was the wrong time to develop the project
"I suppose"
Couldn't get her to bid on me
For she loaned her funds to someone else
He misappropriated the finances
That carpenter continued to skim from the top
Bleeding dry that time and talents
That she could have provided for me

I wrote her a note...
Sealed it with a kiss
Addressed it with love
USPS returned it to sender
"There wasn't enough postage to deliver to her consciousness"
Didn't know then
That the carpenter moonlighted as the mailman
Digging through her letters
Scanning what he wanted her to read
"Fuck you Mister..."
"You won't hide her from me"
But I didn't know that then
So, kept on writing

I wrote her a note...
Many in fact
Disguised as poetry
An even through my simple similes
She can't see me
Metaphorically and literally
She dances around my hyperboles
Quivering behind the knees
Thinking she hears the heart beat through the commas

Filling my spaces with hers
Attaching feelings with words with the aid of emoticons
Going above and beyond
To express the closeted strain

I wrote her a note...
I wrote her a note...
I wrote her a note...
And the only response rendered back
Is her clicking the "LIKE" button...
By accident

Dark Safety

Linger in the bush of former lovers
Smell your residue
Wallow in chalk stained passion
Left in the walls of she victims
Smear your prints in the notebook of my obsession
Not fearing transgressions
Needing to get close enough
For that one shot of you

Wiretap pin punched numbers of your emotional security
Hotline to the sole line in your consciousness
Can't *69 it
Will ring back to your phone jack
I'm always tuned into you

Postal
Doorbells rung
To sing the lyrics of unmarked mail
Sending parcels
Sealed with scented melodies of us
Wanting disappearance
Try returning to sender
Appears on steps once more
I sent it through you
To you
For us

Gated in the community of your sanity
Locked and arm guarded
Thought you found safety in bolted locks
"I never had to break down the security system"
Had keys made as I stroked your next move
Welded to the groove of your comfort zone
Submit to this
It's the escape needed to end the cycle

The Answer is No!

When
Your
Plane
Takes
Off
Leaving the runway
Elevating a new altitude to your future
Will
You
Gaze
Back?

And not take these moments for granted
Not look at them as vivid dalliances
To paint colorful scenes for your memory
Not an experimental portrait
That dangles from the wall
For your guest to gawk
And question its origin
The muse
That infused
The pockets to purchase such artwork

When
Your
Plane
Takes
Off
Leaving the runway
Elevating a new altitude to your future
Will you gaze back?

And desire to stay…

No Security Deposit

Dear Fool:

If this is a vacancy,
And love doesn't live here anymore,
Why are you still paying rent?

Love Poem

Write a love poem
Asked over and over
To place pen to paper
Highlight a grey emotion
In shades of red and pink
Hues of *"love you's"*
"Peek-a-boo's"
And *"I need you's"*
Won't play the fool
In love
Again
First encounter wasn't legit
Held a tight grip on a feeling
That's unsure if it is authentic
Write a love poem
Love
Only validated when the cherub
Armed with bow and arrow
Strike the un-like-ables
To meet
Greet
The *"I'll show you mine"*
"If you show me yours"
Tour of the presentation
To get to the fornication
For the day
Play roles
Humor the humors
The femurs
Any body part
Willing to contribute to the commercialism
Only to get caught up in the VD
STD
Or STI
For those willing to hold on to their pride

Of being swindled
With coated chocolate hearts
The petals of the rose
Placed on sheets of satin
Knowing full well
This celebration is only a buffer
To St. Patrick
The rainbow with golden pots
Green tainted beer
Followed by the bunny
That distributes eggs
Or Passover
For those who follow the "Good Book"
Write a love poem
Asked over and over
To place pen to paper
Highlight a grey emotion
In shades of red and pink
Hues of *"love you's"*
"Peek-a-boo's"
And *"I need you's"*
But the day that happens
A text message
Will be sent
To you
To meet me
At the clinic too
Because we got caught up
In the VD of it all

4 a.m. Mind Spin

Can't
Think
Straight
Nestling
Between
Sheets
Naked
Hoping
Covers
Imitate
Smooth
Caresses
Left
Upon
Breasts
Fondling
All
Night
Until
Next
Day
Working
Overtime
Who
Knew
Payday
Would
Cum
Days
Earlier

Love Notes

God looks out for children
…and fools…
So in hanging out with you
I will never have salvation

The Rest is Unwritten

Seeping into the bowels of depression
Found you at the center
The purgatory
The Hell
On Earth
And the Afterlife
The aftermath of understanding
Over-standing
And misunderstanding the principles of reality
Seeking more
In the gray area
"Nothing can ever be black and white with you"

Wat Da Fux

Cried over you
The first time red veins
Pumped blue blood
A deep navy hue
That struck organs and muscles to create the saline solution
Rushing rapidly through the body
Internal tissues trying to buffer the emotion
An epic fail
Filled with water
Feelings escape through tear ducts to display the sadness for the outside

Cried under you
Believing that the soul was safe in your embrace
Swaddled tenderly in blankets that felt like love
Mended in the belief that this was relief
Was incorrect
Sensed you slither to the arms of another
Gazed longingly as you elevated to distant coordinates
Listened to you deteriorate in the moans of strangers
Stroking us away

Cried next to you
In tandem
Elicited same thoughts and reactions
One soul inhabiting two bodies
Perfection's illusion
A flaw
Leaving the duo a solo tragedy
Afraid to journey onward
Becoming a hermit to oneself
Tears flood the membrane
Drowning the soul in memories

Cried over you

Exhausted energy
Can no longer do it for another
Even after pouring the heart to you
You don’t have a clue

USED 2.0

Rapacity
One
Of
The
Deadly
Sins
Scripted
On
Your
Thigh
Lusting
For
A
Piece
Of
The
Action
This
Sinner
Lacks
Peradventure
Settling
For
Sloth
Instead

Wade in the Water

Lay beside the still water
These breast need to feel gentle palm's caress
Make ripples
In this stagnant life source
Force urgency with every sway
Bathe in the existence provided
Breathe life
As submerged head
Between legs
Blow bubbles to ignite the passion that once was
Create a tide
Back and forward stroking
Turning still pond
Into the Nile
With every flowing essence
Birth within new creations
Show God that He is not the only one to make miracles

The Haiku

Even after I
fuck-ed you, you would never
get the fucking point

Bark Back, Dare U

Peed on your tree
Golden shower erasing partner's fingertips
Momentarily lick the penal process
Until emissions pass the orgasmic tender loins of this guilt trip
To fly high
Is an understatement
Statutes engraved in sheets
Inked thrice over
Quilling this deed into memory
For when you moan
Her vaginal lining secretes my DNA…

She

Masturbation
Is for those who truly love themselves
So, She
Can never reach the depth of her soul
To stroke it to satisfaction
So, She
Will never know what it means
To be cum-pletely happy
For She relies on He
He will never
Can never
Make her lips grin
So when She fakes a smile
He wears a crown of lies
And caresses a scepter of deception
She…
Wishes to debunk his throne
But gave him reign
So She
Will never know what it means
To be cum-pletely happy
Until She strokes her soul
In the face of He
And He jesterly accepts his new title as
Accessory

Piano & Bass

Hitting high notes in the key of G
Spot-ting differences to create a cacophony
Within the symphony to simply
Cum
Drowning out the thunderous applause of the thighs
Hide behind the dripping notes
Oozing satisfaction
Through finger tips
Having a cyber skin blush
Wishing it was the index and middle digit
Dialing up the cervix
Scaling
Beating
Screaming
Skeeting in Morse code
"Some Orgasmic Shit"
Flipped inside out
Outside in
This sin is something to die for
Will spend afterlife times in torment
For the thoughts to repeat again
Collaboration unfinished
Wanting to be plucked once more
The encore is overdue

Stand Firm

Yelling from across the crowded room
Can hear it screaming...

I'm the promises you make and break
I'm what your fantasies call reality
I'm the jealous nature that roots in the soul
I'm your free-will bound with endless obstacles
I'm all or nothing
I'm nothing at all
I'm the unpaid bills
I'm the tears on pillows
I'm the ups and downs
I'm the secrets in the dark
I'm the truth in the light
I'm the in-between
I'm the definite indefinite
I'm the whispered sweet nothings
I'm all that can be lost
I'm all that is found

I am what I am.

And from across the crowded room
Yell from muffled megaphone...

I do! I can!

After a series of "huh's" and "what's"
Push through
Stand face to face
Repeat
And wait…

Queen: Before Thrown Erosion

...She takes me back...

Time traveling through her fallopian tubes-back to where folks lost, their cotton-pickin minds fighting to broom jump into her bloodline-leaving residue on cottonseeds to breed ecstasy

...She takes me back...

Her Hershey dipped mahogany smile has the feet aching to civil march to her consciousness, needing her 1963 to rock me to a new millennium-whisper spiritual somethings to my soul so when our hymnals collide a new gospel is formed-have her freedom ring in my backbone vibrations backbreaking spinal tapping away historical inaccuracies mending the gap in our generational divide

...She takes me back...

To the schooling untaught in classrooms for fear of an European downfall-fingering through archives, found Maat between leatherette sheets-scream your name *"Hatshepsut make me sweat"*- having our passion flood Kemet-secrete oasis that Moses can't part-the Nile, now blushing wishing it back and forward stroked through us-shaking and quaking-we survived the Continental drift

...She takes me back...

And want to live lifetimes in her script-make August Wilson envy that he didn't pen "we"-be the notes that Sarah Vaughan wish she could sing-be the ground underground rap stood on-wrapping tightly in hip's hopping be-bop swaying until we croon spoon through each others rhythm and blues

...She takes me back...

With her epic present steadying pace on a new school track-hoping to avoid demons in the crack of her thrown-having this royal relationship bandage past dynasties

…Wish I were back…

To when she first knew love so, we would never rule in denial…

Chapter Four

The Lyrics of Growth

Diggin' Your Style

The adulation between us
Is deeper than the oceans bottom
Deeper than intimacy
Deeper than the words "I Love Thee"
Deeper than making babies
You see
We fit
Nothing like Nintendo's nonsense
Extending beyond the box of reason
Making time skip seasons
For we are a lifetime
Letting parchment be the prophylactic
That keeps our emotions safe
As we continually stroke each other's hearts with the pen
Pinning the past with present
Ensuring the longevity of the future
You are the cynosure
Erasing the before
And having after bring their 'A' game
You are the basis
For this sis to keep breathing
So thank you for this friendship

Tankashane

Understanding me
Letting moments consume time
We complete the space

Thank you for loving me so
Thank you for loving me so!

Poet's Plea

Never thought
That you would be in my vocabulary
Never thought
My vocabulary could expand
Boosting itself
To swirl
Churn
And burn up the esophagus
Like repeating indigestion
Not liking to vomit
Let it sit
Between the soft and hard palette
A lingual "time out"
Till time ran out
Spilling the words
"I"
"Need"
"You
"In"
"My"
"Life"...

More Than a Rendezvous*

Can't look me in the eye
Can you
Do you love living your lie?

Gazing deeply as the sunsets on an empty orifice, you call a soul
Fabricated tissues
Masking reality with the stench of your denial
You've succumb to repetitious actions eluding cosmetic comfort
Brimstone raging flames screaming to be set free
Symbolizing the truth, you won't devour
Promenading fallacies
Sweetly colored and laced in the stitching of the umbrella you carry
A high-rise soapbox
Merely a stain on your white gloved insecurities
Pretentiously masturbating society into believing your deceit
Making them secrete
Venomous cum
Completely mind fucked by your trickery
Complicating the ones who know true love regardless of form
But you are suave
Smooth talking
Allowing others to believe you are common
Ejaculating your fiction betwixt my fingers
I lapped the tale dry
Mourning the residue
It's the closest I can get to you
Yet still can't pretend that part of me does not exist
My magic is not as strong as yours

Can't look me in the eye
Can you
Do you love living your lie?

Writhing in agony
Stop posting your guilt with self-hatred thorns inside me

Dwelling in your tickle dick tragedy
Ever considered how I felt
How can you resurrect ones soul?
Wallow in the blessing
Encase it back into the tomb
And tell it to wait for another miracle
You didn't mean to save me
Screwed me six ways to Sunday
Never to rise again
Looked to you as my healer
Surprisingly denied the revolutions to relieve this Jack-in-the-box
That was the problem
I am and you are a Jill
Tumbling
Tumbling
Tumbling
…until…
Smashed back into the plastic cell
Confined to the dark spaces of your mind
Bars barricading four cornered illusions
Awaiting a child like innocence
Trust, an entity I no longer see
Blurred visions masquerading as confusion
Blinded by your inconsistencies

Can't look me in the eye
Can you
Do you love living your lie?

Time ticking away
Molasses minutes piling more questions
That slit wrists can no longer answer
Emotions tangled in your essence
Leaving me breathless
Wishing I could stress less
But I am all wound up
Alarmed by the twisted dance we did

To some degree still do
Can't shake this uneasy feeling
Watching you prostitute other connections to avoid my gaze
Stop!
Take a moment to capture my existence
Titanically, seeking rationale from your cerebral blueprint
You've become the pollutant that won't sieve from my body
Penetrated so deeply, rotting my roots ceasing sprouts of clarity
I need not suffer anymore, but you

Can't look me in the eye
Can you
Do you love living your lie?

Without me

**from Sugar Lumps and Black Eye Blues © 2007, edited for this publication*

Reprised Rendezvous

Look me in the eye
Won't you
Let me tell you why

This is the reprise
Time to turn the table on its side
Before the bucket list
Becomes an epitaph
Sending you
My apologies

Loved to quick
Expecting new emotions to stick
To prove
To you
That I could feel again
Condemned
Your honesty
To the shackles of my insecurities
Slaved-shipped the relationship
Had you jump over board
To save the sanity
Of a generated bondage
Used wordplay
As a hide-a-way
Scapegoat-ing
The fact
That I too
Cooked up drama
Marinated it in pity
Sautéed it in sympathy
Garnished it with guilt
Served it on a silver platter of mindless majesty
Let you hold burden's flavor in my words
The master chef

Of verbal destruction
Trying to stop
But the elephant is in the room
Pretend not to see it
Yet poke and prod it
With inside jokes
And whispered undertones

Look me in the eye
Won't you
Let me tell you why

This is the reprise
Time to turn the table on its side
Before the bucket list
Becomes an epitaph
Sending you
My apologies

Resurrected love
After a three day grace
Struck the tomb
To make room
For you to be heaven sent
Something a human could never be
Forced fallacies
Scrutiny
Hypocrisy
When the whole time
Should have been loving me
Lesson learned
A tad too late
Took the luxury in hating you
Pinned down your essence
Dug and scraped into your soul
Excavated nothingness
Couldn't make you love me

The self needed to posses
Now stressed
Stuck in a land of “Used To’s”
Bound in the jackets of “He Should’s”
Wrestled us to the “Must To’s”
And you
Flew away
Before I could state the claim
The reason
For being temporarily insane
I was the blame
Retrospect
Had me bouncing emotional checks
Withdrew more than your deposit
Making fraudulent thoughts
Accumulating fees
Interest rates
That even fate
Can’t help dissipate
With common sense
I was the sin
Thank you for not giving in

Look me in the eye
Won’t you
Let me tell you why

This is the reprise
Time to turn the table on its side
Before the bucket list
Becomes an epitaph
Sending you
My apologies

Random Thought

Poetry
is more
intimate than
stroking your
private place

Royal Disappointment

So you caught me on a weak day…

A week day
A humped day
A bump in which you strapped the flesh down
Flipped it over
Said *"take it anyway, don't get too bold"*
Took my bush
Served it alfresco with an umbrella-ed cocktail
Arranged it so it could be poked and prodded
On display for the nation to perceive as slipshod
Slap dashed
Sprinkled with recklessness
A public disturbance
Since you told me my essence is not my own
This nature rests fruitless on bed of tainted greens
Baring nothing but bad news
Turning hard labor into propaganda
Left un-mirandized and serving the time regardless
You treat suicide bombers with more respect
Suppose I should have done it for Allah
The only name spoken in the bed sheets
Where you and I once played
Now, having my blankets cover another lover
More than one time
Even when they're in your day dreams
They're fucking your mind
Deduce that next time will be different

But you caught me on a weak day…

A week day
A humped day
A bump in which you tried to smooth out with lies
Deceit covered your fingers tips

Stroking uneasiness into my soul
Co-horsing negative energy to pretend it's an apology
Telling me is only butterflies that make me shutter so
Should have known you were dangerous
"It's the quiet ones to watch out for"
For not following mama's advice
The price paid
Lies rancid in the seat of my consciousness
Let you in
Let you dive head first
Into me
Filling the spaces that DNA could not auto-correct
So, yes
I expect more from you

But you caught me on a weak day…

A week day
A humped day
A bump in which you pounded out like a needless pimple
A blackhead
A black head I let submerge into my virginity
Those purest thoughts can never be refunded
Left with store credit's imagination for the future
Forcing me to buy from your store
Having poor pockets
Window shopping ensembles of freedom
Knowing well in advance
The next paycheck won't clear
For it was signed away years ago
The scarlet pussy's signature
Stroked the death sentence of my growth
Everything has been bouncing since

For you caught me on a weak day…

A week day

A humped day
A bump in the road you hurled over despite the yield signs
Attempting to run the yellow light
You succeeded briefly
But even on this weak day
This week day
This humped day
The bump is no longer me
Places switched
I run first place
While you bring up the rear
Location that should have been your original stance
In the back
Back of mind's sight
Back
Back to the moment where there was no light
Until a GOD flipped a switch
Noticing for the first time
You would always be my downfall
And this weak day
This week day
This humped day
The bump
Mound of uselessness
Is no longer this Queen

Honesty

Need to make these emotions tangible
It's not about the physical
Our minds have been fornicating for years
Her cerebral
My cortex
Share a vortex all their own
Slipping in and out of sound bytes, internet waves and Sim chips
This friendship
Is deeper than any biological kinship
But the body wants a piece of what the mind has experienced for years
It's the simple creature
Needing a physical blueprint to display what the hype is about
It's not about fucking her because we are too old for that
It's about the discovery
The exploration
Without Sprint Navigation
Using the index fingers to map new routes into her soul
Want to lick her until she cums 1,000 times in my mouth
Swallow her sweet nectar so the next time I secrete it's her DNA
She is closer to me than the dermis layers that blanket my muscles and tissue
The issue
We can never be in love like that

We dwell with the simile and metaphor alone
Her pen
My pad
A clad pair of instruments
Strumming in tandem
To polyrhythmic pentameters
Of consonants and vowels
Stroking notebook spines
With rhyme
Sublime Haikus

Free verse
Bits of Prose, too
Always wanting to hum to her tune
But we can never be in love like that

The physicality will make me weaker
Already sprung
When her tongue
Utters nouns, verbs and adjectives
The imagery in her poetic symmetry
Make my daydreams
Wet dreams
And I cream to the possibility of her in my imagination
But we can never be in love like that

The fact
Don't feel worthy enough
Working diligently to complete the path
Before dashing to pull on her heartstring
Taking the time to fill myself up
To be whole without her
Want our essences to compliment
A supplement
Not bandage past wounds
She is everything seen for my future
Crave to place my heart on speakerphone
To shout
"I'm out, I'm out"
"I'm want to be queer with her"
Near to her
Formulate seed in her womb
Caramelizing our connection
Off-springing each other's presence
Growing old
Basking in stories told and forgotten
But we can never be in love like that

Too shy to tell her
Fearful
Near tear; full of anxiety
Propriety holds the reigns
As Lust tries to intertwine the four-letter word
"L"
That chokes the throat
"O"
The four-letter word that remains hostage by the soft palette and lesioned heart
"V"
The four-letter word beckons me
"E"
"Say me"
"Say me"
"You know you want me"
"Don't hide from me, do it for her"
The punk in me won't take the risk
Not wanting to open again
Believing her essence will change all that
Diving head first into uncharted nothingness
I sign to myself
"I want you inside me"
In hopes that each hand motion
Acts as a carrier pigeon to her psyche
Aching to be the afterthought in her mind
The sway in her strut
The shimmer in her hair
To release from this emotional rut
Completely stuck
Longing
Can we ever be in love like that?

Tit4Tat

Took the ink off the page
Siphoned it onto my arm
To remind me
Remind me that I allowed you to create tears
Inside my left chamber
Flooded it so rapidly
That when it burst
It reminded me
Reminded me that you swaddled my torso
With yours
Making the first time so electric
We couldn't even finish
This reminded me
Reminded me that
That as I was falling deeper into the understanding
Of what "we" were
I awoke with the letter formations folded in quarters
Detailing nothing, I could decipher
Everything about it spelled "Dear John"
But I was a Jill not thrilled
Unmoved and devastated
This reminded me
Reminded me that the pain was so unbearable
Took to easing the pressure with lancets of reasoning
Snuggling in crimson comfort
This reminded me
Reminded me that you called five times that day
Saving me from myself
Maybe you felt me slipping away
Couldn't say then that you loved me
But it reminded me
Reminded me that I never thanked you properly
Because I was vexed
Peeved you'd leave for someone who wouldn't cherish you
Like I could

Like I wanted to
Like I wished to
Like I craved to
This reminded me
Reminded me that you did leave
Left me to resort to extreme Virgo tendencies
Worry so deeply that most nights
Needed to weep to sleep
Pray to make it through the day
That you were truly OK
This reminded me
Reminded me when you finally text me
I kept it for years
And I would have the text still
If my old phone hadn't kicked the bucket
This reminded me
Reminded me that I never wanted to lose you again
So, I took the ink off the page
Siphoned it onto my arm
To hold forever
Hold the you
That was more than a best friend…

AFTERWARD

***

"Silence: The Cuffs That No Longer Bind"

Afterwards..., I am left, as all readers will be, to answer the question, "What do you think? How have you just experienced **Mahogany Nectar**?" Despite taking, multiple dives into the pool of thoughts and feelings of TS Hawkins - weaving and bobbing in and out of her seemingly innermost thoughts, I still found myself with ideas that were in a constant state of motion. Such motion has left me both perplexed and challenged to capture the words that will formulate an offering that is as generous as what Hawkins has shared throughout the pages of **Mahogany Nectar**.

To know the author and to read her words posed a challenge because I know a little something about her story. Hawkins' poetry has provided her with the ability to unlock and unleash her fears, her frustrations, "instincts...," her desire and willingness to love and to be loved – but not at all cost. I knew a little something about that. As such, for me, reading her work became an exercise that required a specific ability. I had to stretch. This stretching involved placing what I thought I knew along the sideline – and allowing those thoughts to function as mere spectators while I, the unknowing reader, prepared to take in everything **Mahogany Nectar** was preparing to offer. Allow me to bring you to the beginning of my process.

I wanted a definition. I started with the title. When I think of "Mahogany", I think of an exotic moderate reddish brown wood that is valued for its strength as well as its beauty. When I considered "Nectar", I wanted to go deeper – remembering, according to Greek Mythology, it [nectar] was the "Life-giving drink of the Gods"; something strong and beautiful that breeds new life and is cyclical – constantly evolving. I wanted to place the two meanings together, if only to provide me with a better sense of why Hawkins chose

Mahogany Nectar as her title. I mean, the title was catchy and seductive enough that it would make a prospective reader look twice, but what was it really all about? Was **Mahogany Nectar** both symbolic and literal – referencing the beauty and strength that is a component of her culture and/or her personal experience? I quickly realized, in order to answer the question, I had to move beyond the title and connect with the words on the pages.

As my journey began, it was not hard to figure out that **Mahogany Nectar** was going to be a compilation of *"Outspoken"* moments. That description [OutSpoken] intentionally borrowed from a poem of the same name in chapter two's <u>Soap Box Auction Blocked</u> captures the essence of this body of work. As the poem concludes, *"silence is no longer the cuffs that bind"*, although this specific piece references a violation and a resolve to reclaim power, it encompasses the ferocity of her attitude and determination to be the proverbial captain of her own ship. Each chapter seems to represent a different component of her life. From chapter one where she is <u>Leaving the Nursery</u> in full awareness of a deficit of love, to chapter four <u>The Lyrics of Growth</u> where she is able to clearly articulate gratitude for the love she has received. Hawkins remains in both a constant state of search and rescue as she writes, *"So, if I have to stalk my past to find my future, then that is what I need to do."* This line from chapter one's *Discovery* captures her modus operandi made clear through the reflective nature of several pieces. As the saying goes, "Hindsight is 20/20" and Hawkins is looking back with eyes that can see the past, present and hopes for the future. She refuses to be *Invisible* and inaudible – without a voice – *"through the paper and pen I [she] breathe[s] again."* **Mahogany Nectar** breathes like new life grasping for air and the ability to live without assistance. It shows gratitude for this life and as such, refuses to remain silent. It represents a release that unveils a reincarnated fearless superhero that recognizes the beauty within; and will write about a strong wrong without worry.

There is sadness. *Wind Blades* left me questioning and recalling the disappointment that arises when you give with an open heart and receive nothing in return. However, that sadness does not steer the ship or determine the journey. It simply makes the road traveled even and known. The bumps in the road are par-for-the-course and oppose to cause for retreat. *Colored In the Box* represents lessons learned early that revolved around knowing your place and staying there. However, her journey revealed more to the story and a realization that there was something more to believing [without question], in what you were told. The wisdom that comes with her experiences provided Hawkins with the ability to see the real story and believe it.

What have you – what have I learned about **Mahogany Nectar**? Our lessons are going to be relative to our experience. If you are like me, and you believe in the power of the human spirit – then you may be reflecting on the richness that is within and the power that comes with our ability to heal. Perhaps it has left you questioning your *Dinner with Truth* and your *"xeroxed wisdom"*. Perhaps you are still simply pondering the lessons and are preparing to re-experience and savor the words like sweet saccharine that titillates the taste buds. Then again, this is poetry; and isn't that what it is supposed to do? Shouldn't poetry leave readers to continue their own conversation? Isn't poetry the tool that has the ability to break through and reveal an author's truth in an absolute and succinct fashion; and yet help readers to discover their own [truth]? Some of the poems were short and straight to the point. Brevity did not reduce the power of the words. The quick wit and careful intonations can turn the words into a song you remember. A song that introduces itself to your spirit and together they marvel in the thoughts and ideas that has somehow awakened senses a person may have been neglecting for years. In this case, the song I hope you remember is **Mahogany Nectar**.

Keisha L. Johnson, M.Ed

ABOUT THE AUTHOR

***

"Words, Verses and New Chapters"

TS Hawkins is the daughter of two New Jersey educators who watched their three-year-old prance around in her underpants singing to Michael Jackson! Containing the zany energy into performing and writing, Hawkins adds author, vocalist and performance poet to her résumé. Ironically enough, she still dances around in her underpants to Michael Jackson. Some things never change ☺

When she is on breaks from the **Authors Under 30 Book Tour**, she performs and promotes literacy in public schools. As a youth, many teachers and mentors helped foster her talents so she enjoys the opportunity to give back to the community whenever possible. Upping the communal outreach ante, she is to be published in *Verseadelphia: an Anthology of Philadelphia's African American Poets and Spoken Word Artists during the 20th -21st Century*. She is elated that this publication will be a learning tool for the Philadelphia public school system. *Verseadelphia* is to be published by New City Press. Crowned the *PBGP Poetry Slam Champion* in 2009, she is excited that her work is taking shape and inspiring individuals from all lifestyles.

A Temple University Poetry as Performance Alumni, Hawkins completes her round of saccharine glazed trilogy with *Mahogany Nectar*. Its cohorts *Sugar Lumps and Black Eye Blues* and *Confectionately Yours* have had rave reviews in print and radio media. It is with hope *Mahogany Nectar*, *Lil Black Book: All The Long Stories Short* and her new teen publication *Black Suga: diary of a troublesome teenager* will follow in the latter books' successes. Selections from her books have been featured on: 107.9 WRNB (*Whispers in the Dark with Tiffany Bacon)*, LP Spoken Word Tour, Brown Girl Radio: *a Cure for the Common*, Da Block, WRTI 90.1 FM (*The Bridge with J. Michael Harrison*), Studio Luna, Improv Café, Temple University, Aspire Arts, NBC 10, Moonstone: 100 Poets Reading, NateBrown Entertainment, The Liacouras Center,

Tree House Books, The Bowery, Warmdaddy's, Jus Words, NJ Performing Arts Center, T Bar, Verbal Roots, The NAACP, The REC, Lyrical Playground, Lincoln University, The Pleazure Principle, Bar 13, Robin's Bookstore, umuvme Radio, First Person Arts, The RED Lounge for AIDS Awareness, Women's Ink, Lady M Events, The Painted Bride, So 4Real Charis Books and Dr. Sonia Sanchez Literacy Night. Next, she is trying her hand at playwriting!

In the meantime she produces her own radio at PR Radio Station. Hawkins also writes for *If You Give A Girl A Pen*, a blog that gives woman writers a positive forum to enhance writing fundamentals!

For bookings and detailed information:
www.TSPoetics.com